Under Siege:
10 Questions Every School Board Member Should Ask

KEN ODOM, JR.

If

BY RUDYARD KIPLING

If you can keep your head when all about you
Are losing theirs and blaming it on you,
If you can trust yourself when all men doubt you,
But make allowance for their doubting too;
If you can wait and not be tired by waiting,
Or being lied about, don't deal in lies,
Or being hated, don't give way to hating,
And yet don't look too good, nor talk too wise:

If you can dream—and not make dreams your master;
If you can think—and not make thoughts your aim;
If you can meet with Triumph and Disaster
And treat those two impostors just the same;
If you can bear to hear the truth you've spoken
Twisted by knaves to make a trap for fools,
Or watch the things you gave your life to, broken,
And stoop and build 'em up with worn-out tools:

If you can make one heap of all your winnings
And risk it on one turn of pitch-and-toss,
And lose, and start again at your beginnings
And never breathe a word about your loss;
If you can force your heart and nerve and sinew
To serve your turn long after they are gone,
And so hold on when there is nothing in you
Except the Will which says to them: 'Hold on!'

If you can talk with crowds and keep your virtue,
Or walk with Kings—nor lose the common touch,
If neither foes nor loving friends can hurt you,
If all men count with you, but none too much;
If you can fill the unforgiving minute
With sixty seconds' worth of distance run,
Yours is the Earth and everything that's in it,
And—which is more—you'll be a Man, my son!

Table of Contents

History teaches us that groups under siege normally meet a bad end. Often, it seems like public education is under siege. There is only one way to respond.

The locally elected school board is a uniquely American institution whose roots stretch back to the earliest foundations of our political system. Most countries do not govern education in this decentralized manner. In order to understand how to effectively use its power, the school board must first understand why it has the power in the first place.

A position on the school board is a volunteer role that entails long hours, high visibility, and tremendous pressure. Yet, many school board members have trouble articulating why they would willingly take on this responsibility. Understanding what prompted you to run for the school board points to where time and effort should be spent.

A school district without vision is like a blind folded person trying to cross a crowded room. Most districts will never move from where they are today. They will make helpless noises and look with shock upon the difficult task that they have inherited. Those that do move may shuffle in the wrong direction, paying attention to irrelevant or unhelpful indicators. If, by chance, a district happens to move in the right direction it will often focus too narrowly, reaching out with its arms to avoid crashing into something. No such district survives without bumps, bruises, and scars.

VI.   Does what you measure matter?   39

School board members are busy individuals. We are volunteers and, as such, we are heckled and harried and have numerous and diverse responsibilities outside of the education realm. We simply cannot afford to be distracted by anything that does not advance our core calling to have a vision for kids.

VII.   Do you demonstrate commitment to education improvement?   46

School board members are granted the gift of touching eternity. The work they do today will echo through the generations and pave the way for the continuance of our culture. If they fail to demonstrate true commitment, as evidenced by allotting meaningful time to consideration of critical dimensions of student achievement, that gift will be sacrificed.

VIII.   Do you prioritize leadership development?   51

Leadership can be – must be – taught. Leadership is a skill that is developed through practice and focused discipline. Like other skills, there may be some who are born with traits that make that skill easier to master. But, possession of those traits does not guarantee mastery any more than the lack of those traits condemns one to failure.

IX.   Is your board united?   57

There is no place for personal agendas in this most critical of leadership tasks. Stakeholders will not rally behind a divided board. And the board needs stakeholders to help execute its vision.

X.   Do you take advantage of your resources?   62

The school board is armed with an impressive assortment of tools. These tools, when used in support of a compelling vision within a leadership framework, are truly transformative. Indeed, they are among the most powerful tools that any local leader could hope to wield.

Great movements require spokespeople who can communicate with and represent the values of the people they serve. Of all of the groups who claim an interest in education and education improvement, only one would seem to unite all of the prerequisites to fill this role - members of local school boards.

Professional football great Peyton Manning once noted that there are two types of people in the world: people who make things happen and people who wonder what just happened. Too many school boards are wondering what happened - to local control, to the education agenda, to the future direction of our nation's youth.

Author's Note

As of this writing, I am mid-way through my tenth year of service on my local school board in Tomball, Texas. During that time, I've had the opportunity to work with and to meet any number of dedicated, passionate, caring individuals. Most of these people have good ideas, are thoughtful about education, and truly care about kids.

That's why I am continually baffled that local school boards do not feature more prominently in the debates about education reform. For the most part, school boards are either viewed as impediments to meaningful change or, worse, summarily dismissed as irrelevant to the conversation. How is it, I've wondered, that such a large group of politically powerful and passionately motivated people can be so easily marginalized?

The answer, I think, is that we have allowed it to happen. As I note in the chapters to follow, we board members make our critics' jobs easier by focusing on the mundane instead of the meaningful. I hope that this volume serves as catalyst to awaken the sleeping giant.

This work has grown out of a presentation that was first given in the summer of 2012 at a Texas Association of School Boards conference. The thoughts reflected here have been honed by a number of follow up presentations, conversations with thought leaders, a regular blog feature, and some old-fashioned reflection.

I owe much and more to the many board members, school district administrators, teachers, and advocates who have listened to me and offered their views. In particular, Dr. Richard Griffin has been a mentor and an inspiration. My fellow Tomball ISD board members have largely modeled what I think of as "right" board behavior. I am particularly indebted to Kathy Handler and Mark Lewandowski for their thoughtful reading of the initial draft of this work. I was finally motivated to finish this book because of my participation in Leadership TASB, led by Dr. Bill Rutherford. Fellow Leadership TASB member Amy Hays provided another critical eye during the editing process.

As I concluded the effort, it occurred to me that certain teachers, family members, and friends from my youth now provide the voice for the thoughts that I put down on paper. My dad is the model of persistence and determination that enabled me to keep coming back to this project. Margaret Goode, my high school English teacher, and David Kay, my high school speech and debate coach, had as much to do with my written and spoken voice as anyone. And my neighbor the postman, Otis Walker, provides the admonishment to continually seek improvement and to use my gifts in the service of others.

Finally, but most importantly, I must say thanks to God for my wife, Traci. She has had to listen to me rattle on for nearly 18 years. I'm sure she appreciates sharing some of that burden with you.

Ken Odom
The Woodlands, TX
February 13, 2014

Prologue

Under Siege

Siege [seej] – (noun) The act and process of surrounding a fortified place in such a way as to isolate it for the purpose of lessening the resistance of the defenders and thereby making capture possible.

I am a big fan of history. I love to learn about the issues, conflicts, decisions, and relationships that have shaped the way in which we relate to today's world. I believe, like many others, that the lessons of the past can help us to better navigate the future.

Recently, many of my history studies have included military confrontations. The combination of strategy and luck that determines the victor in these disputes makes for fascinating reading. One particular type of battle has really gotten my attention – the siege.

A siege normally occurs when a larger, better funded army meets with a smaller army that does not enjoy access to as many resources as its foe. Instead of risking open battle, the smaller army will sometimes decide to run away and hide in some place that seems, at the time, to be safe. Typically this safe place is a heavily fortified sanctuary from which the smaller army hopes to wait out the larger army. Maybe they'll get bored…or distracted…or tired. The hope is that the larger army will eventually fade away and that the smaller army will have survived the encounter.

Besides heavy fortifications, sieges share a few additional characteristics. Often, the besieged army begins to suffer. Physically, they may experience a lack of food and water that gradually wears at the endurance of the soldiers. Mentally, the army must fight against boredom. Socially, there may be internal dissension – remember the arguments that you and your siblings had when you were forced to share the back seat on a long family road trip! Spiritually, the besieged army rapidly loses its will to fight. Surrender becomes a more attractive option when victory is not visible.

The most striking shared characteristic, though, is the manner in which many sieges end. In my reading it seems that, almost always, a siege ends poorly for the smaller army. Almost always, a siege ends in death and destruction for the besieged.

***

Siege of Jerusalem, 597 BC.

Key Players: Zedekiah (King of Judah), Nebuchadnezzar (King of Babylon)

As punishment for rebellion, the might of the Babylonian empire – the most powerful military might that the world had yet seen - surrounded Jerusalem after Zedekiah's retreat. In the end, Jerusalem was burned to the ground, Solomon's temple was looted, and the priests of the temple – the Levites - were executed. And, in the ultimate act of cruel humiliation, Zedekiah was forced to watch as his sons were executed and then had his eyes poked out. The last thing Zedekiah would ever see was the death of his children.

***

I think that sieges reveal a particularly valuable lesson for those charged with leading public education because, in many ways, public education is under siege. A large army with seemingly endless resources – an army of politicians, professors, unions, non-profits, charter school operators, and others – is arrayed against a small and unique group of diverse and fragmented locally elected individuals. This small group faces an arsenal of funding cuts, mandates, and district takeovers. In response, local public education leaders have increasingly retreated behind fortifications of administrative minutiae.

A brief glance at public education, and especially at the typical local school board, reveals the tell-tale effects of the siege. School board agendas are littered with managerial tasks that are only superficially related to education improvement. Tasks like approving the check register, granting easements, and reviewing field trips dominate valuable board discussion time.

Academic achievement is flat or declining as schools are starved of the critical leadership energies needed to sustain continuous improvement. Internal dissension, in the form of bitter political divisions between and among board members and school administrators, capture the headlines. Obscured by the walls of administrative detail, a clear and consistent vision for education is seemingly impossible. Nestled within the cocoon of management, school boards increasingly lose touch with the citizens who elected them to serve their interests.

Most disturbingly, a negative perception of the school board's value has become the norm amongst those who advocate for education improvement. School boards, it is argued, are not equipped to drive meaningful change. School board activities, it is suggested, are divorced from student achievement. School boards, it is asserted, are increasingly irrelevant in the conversation about improving education.

For proof that these perceptions are pervasive one needs only to listen to any of the many conferences and symposiums held by well-meaning organizations in the hopes of adding to the body of knowledge that will drive education reform. As a marathoner, my training includes a number of long, slow runs on early weekend mornings. This winter, I decided to listen to the recordings of some of these conferences as I trained. I listened to literally hours of reports, studies, and debates about what is ailing education and how it might be cured. In that time, I heard from politicians, policy makers, professors, union leaders, state education administrators, non-profit leaders, and charter school operators. Never once, though, did I hear from those on the front lines of education leadership. Never once did I hear the thoughts of a locally elected school board trustee.

***

Siege of Acre, August 28, 1189 – July 12, 1191 (Third Crusade).

Key Players: King Richard the Lionheart, Saladin.

The Muslim leader Saladin had split his army, with a core group operating from the mountains and a smaller group entrenched near the seaside town of Acre. Of the Holy Land cities, Acre was perhaps best suited to withstand a siege. It was surrounded on three sides by thick stone walls and on the fourth by the sea. The sea route was guarded by a wall that went beneath the water and a tower that commanded the approach of any enemy vessels. Two-thousand seven hundred Muslim soldiers sought Acre's shelter.

Despite surviving numerous assaults by Christian crusaders, Acre eventually fell as the foundation beneath its walls was weakened until the stone collapsed. The city surrendered and all 2,700 Muslim soldiers were executed.

***

What if this set of pervasive beliefs is wrong, though? Research tells us that well-trained and motivated teachers can impact student achievement, and so we focus on teacher preparation and selection. Research suggests that a rich, diverse,

15

and broad curriculum leads to better educational outcomes, so we invest in developing a more comprehensive offering. Research insists that design principles like class size and shape dictate student engagement, so we build new buildings and hire new staff. Yet, in spite of all of this, education still seems stuck in neutral. What if the local school board is, in fact, the missing link in the chain of an education breakthrough?

Far from being irrelevant, the local school board can be a core determinant of student achievement. This is because, even though the school board trustee is not engaged in the day to day effort of direct student engagement, the school board controls the conditions that allow for successful teaching and learning. The school board makes decisions about district leadership, district priorities, accountability, resource allocation, and community engagement. Each of these decisions contributes to the environment in which our students learn and grow.

***

The Alamo, February 23, 1836 – March 6, 1836.

Key Players: General Antonio Lopez de Santa Anna, William B. Travis, Jim Bowie.

Remembered as the glorious catalyst of the war that resulted in Texas' independence, the Alamo was, in fact, a siege. One-hundred eighty-nine Texans took refuge in the Alamo as Santa Anna's 2,000 troops sought to take San Antonio. After a valiant fight, the Alamo was overrun. All 189 Texas fighting men were killed.

***

Recent research, like the Lighthouse Project sponsored by the Iowa Association of School Boards, confirms the link between school board actions and student achievement. In fact, high performing school districts are governed by school boards that are decidedly different – in their beliefs about education and in the ways in which they act on those beliefs – than other school districts. The challenge for the local school board – the path to ending the siege and returning to the offensive in the fight for public education – is to identify those beliefs and actions that appropriately position local leadership in the context of education reform. This book seeks to begin that process by posing ten questions, which can be asked of the individual school board member or of the school board as a body, that reveal areas for further contemplation. At the end of the book, I have included a brief self-assessment tool that can be used to help structure your thinking about these questions. The hope is that school boards will be awakened and revived. As a group, school boards represent a very powerful education constituency. If ever awakened, this giant can lead a renewal of American public education.

Chapter 1

What is the purpose of a school board?

"Local assemblies of citizens constitute the strength of
free nations."
-Alexis de Tocqueville, Democracy in America

In his 2012 book <u>World Class Learners: Educating Creative</u> <u>and Entrepreneurial Students</u>, education professor and author Yong Zhao from the University of Oregon asserts that, broadly speaking, there are "two types of educational systems in the world." The first, and by far the most dominant, is a centralized system. In this system, which is exemplified by countries like China, Singapore, and Korea, a central government authority bears the responsibility for determining what students will learn, how they will learn it, and how that learning will be measured. There is no such thing as local education governance in this model. All of the key decisions are made at the very highest levels of the nation's government.

Far less abundant is a decentralized education system. In a decentralized system, there is little to no national control over the inputs and outputs of education. Instead, local bodies – at the state, community, or even individual school level – determine what education should be and exercise considerable latitude in defining the methods used and the resources available to these efforts. The United States is the embodiment of this type of system.

Stated simply, the locally elected school board is a uniquely American institution whose roots are found in the early citizen's fear of powerful central control. In a very real sense, the local school board is an expression of the Federalism concept on which this nation's government was built. That concept suggests that governing power is best leveraged when in the hands of people who are members of the community. As community members, they are held accountable to those that they represent and are uniquely positioned to understand the wants and needs of the local populace.

Today, precious few remaining governing structures afford the local populace the level of autonomy that the local school board does. The local school board has broad powers to form and implement policies that govern curriculum standards, accountability measures, and resource allocation. Given the school board's global uniqueness, it is worthwhile for us to reflect upon its purpose. Why do we have school boards in the first place?

The answer may lie in the purpose of formal education itself. The twentieth century educator John Dewey argued that formal education arises when the amount of information that must be mastered in order to become a productive member of society grows to such an extent that it becomes necessary to write it down. In other words, as long as one can learn all that he or she needs to know about living in a society by standing in a field while someone collects berries or by hiding behind a rock while someone spears a mastodon, there is very little need for formal education. As soon, though, as there is a need to write things down in order to remember, a need for formal education emerges.

The purpose of formal education, then, is to pass along the collected traditions, values, wisdom, and knowledge whose mastery insures the survival of our culture and our society. We tend to couch this purpose in more practical terms today. We might say that the purpose of education is to get a good job or to be prepared for the ups and downs that life throws our way or to appreciate the wonders of creation, but each of these is just another way of saying that we want to make sure that our society is able to survive and thrive via the prospects of succeeding generations.

Ensuring our culture's survival is a formidable task, and we do not entrust it to just anyone. We certainly would not be comfortable if the work of preserving our traditions, values, and knowledge fell to someone who does not share our unique experiences. Instead, we entrust the survival of this legacy to a group of locally elected representatives whose job is to determine what and how the next generation will learn what they need to know, how that learning will be measured, and when that learning has reached maturity.

The locally elected school board, then, is responsible for fulfilling a stewardship function. Stewardship is the protection of something that is considered worth preserving. That is why we have created school boards – because we believe our culture is worth preserving and we think that it is so important that we will only entrust our culture's survival to those that are immediately familiar with and answerable to us.

The job of insuring that our culture survives has only gotten harder as society has advanced. Things have changed tremendously since Dewey published <u>Democracy and Education</u> in 1915. Today, communication is instant and is everywhere. Every blog, every tweet, every status update, every text, every commercial...all are tiny bits of culture. Consider these facts:

- Former Google CEO Eric Schmidt has said that the amount of information created every two years is greater than the total amount of information created from the dawn of civilization to 2003.
- The amount of information created in one year would fill 37,000 libraries of Congress.
- The amount of information in one newspaper is more than the amount of information a person alive in the 17th century would have encountered in an entire lifetime.

Much of this growth has happened in the last 20 years, and certainly has accelerated in the last sixty or seventy years. That means our society has become more complex during that time. Responding to this underlying cultural change is the charge of the locally elected school board.

The pace of information generation is matched by our abilities to access that information. Twenty years ago, gathering the three statistics above would have required me to:

- Get in the car and drive to the campus of the local university.
- Enter the campus library and proceed to the card catalog, a massive collection of drawers, each filled with hundreds of 3x5 index cards.
- Flip through the cards until finding several that referenced "information."
- Copy the Dewey decimal number that would provide directions to the appropriate stack of books.
- Scan the books until I found a few promising ones.
- Carry those books to a table and flip through page after page, hoping to find a useful statistic.
- Return those books to the shelves and head to the microfiche section.
- Pour over back issues of periodicals on film, hoping to find a useful statistic.

This enterprise could easily consume several hours, if not a full day.

Here is how these statistics were actually found:

- Sitting at a desk at work, I flipped my attention between two monitors. One was showing a Google search page and the other was displaying a presentation being shared from a desktop in India. Scarcely listening to a speaker via conference call through a headset while texting my wife, I found these figures in about 5 minutes.

Today, we all have super computers in our pockets. This means that the ways in which we access and interact with information has changed. Access is not limited to information. Access applies to relationships, too. An unpopular high school kid in the early 1990s may have had 4 or 5 friends. More popular kids had 20 or 30 friends. The most popular of kids might have claimed 200 or 300 friends.

A "typical" kid today has more than 1000 "friends" on Facebook.

True, these are not friends of the sort that most adults understand, but each of those connections represents a relationship. Each of those connections represents a different way of sharing information. Each of those connections represents a different way of learning.

The context of community has changed, too. In today's wired world, a community is more than our neighborhood or town. Ideas and commerce are truly global. Almost every large company, and many smaller companies, has business dealings with overseas customers and partners. Social media allows us to interact instantaneously with people living an ocean away. Political movements in far-flung reaches of the globe have a direct and meaningful impact on our daily lives.

Given this level of change and the evolving nature of what it takes to insure cultural relevance, it is only prudent that we examine critically who we choose to trust with the job of determining what is worth preserving of our culture and values. Some would argue, and with merit, that locally elected bodies are not equipped to engage students at the level of complexity required to enable them to become productive members of a society that looks very little like the society we inhabited just a couple of decades ago. Others assert that the people we should trust most with this daunting challenge are the ones that we know the best – the ones that have a vested interest in the well-being of our immediate surroundings.

No matter how you choose to answer this question, this is a very different way of thinking about the local school board than most people – even local school board members – generally take when considering local school governance. School board service is more than a tax rate, a mascot, or an easement. To serve on a school board is, whether consciously or not, to stake out a position with respect to some of the most critical questions facing any people. How are we to survive as a group? What is our group's place in the world? Will we continue to thrive and flourish? Understanding and appreciating the enormity of and the importance of this task is central to ensuring that the local school board positively impacts student achievement.

Chapter 2

Why did you decide to run for the school board?

"The effectiveness of school board governance is the single most important determinant of school district success or failure."
- Rod Paige

Palo Alto, California is the home of Stanford University, one of the most outstanding institutions of higher learning in the United States. Known as "the Farm" to its students and alumni, Stanford was ranked as the fifth best university in the nation by *U. S. News and World Report* in 2012. This ranking places Stanford among other academic superstars like Harvard, Yale, and MIT. Located in the heart of Silicon Valley, Stanford is home to 22 Nobel laureates, 4 Pulitzer Prize winners, top ranked schools of education and medicine, and the nation's number one ranked graduate school of business. With a ridiculously small 5:1 faculty to student ratio, Stanford has produced diverse and successful alumni like former president Herbert Hoover and golfing legend Tiger Woods.

In recent years, though, Stanford has received more publicity about its football team than its academic accomplishments. The Cardinal finished the 2013 season with a conference championship and an appearance in the Rose Bowl. This was the fourth straight season that Stanford finished with a berth in a Bowl Championship Series game and the program is one of only five teams to have accomplished such a feat. Moreover, Stanford has sent a number of former players into the National Football League, including standout quarterback Andrew Luck and Super Bowl champion Richard Sherman.

Stanford's football successes would have been difficult to predict based on the first seven years of this century. During that time, Stanford won an average of four games per year and cycled through three different coaches. The lowest point of their football futility was reached in 2006, when the Cardinal won only one game while losing eleven and finished dead last in the Pac-10 conference. Stanford was, quite literally, one of the worst college football programs in the country.

In 2007, Stanford began the journey that would take them from laughingstock to juggernaut. That year, Stanford fans found a reason for hope as the team quadrupled its win total. The upward climb had begun, and the Cardinal added wins each year until, in 2010, Stanford – lowly Stanford – won 12 games against only one defeat and tasted victory in the postseason for the first time in 16 years.

How did they do it? Stanford University did not lower its academic standards so that the school could admit a few elite athletes to the program. Fewer than 6% of applicants are admitted to "the Farm." More than half of Stanford applicants have a perfect 4.0 grade point average and 80% of them were ranked in the top 10% of their high school class. One out of every 7 applicants for admission posts a perfect score on the math section of the SAT.

Stanford did not drop down into a lesser conference. For much of recent history, Stanford was a member of the Pac-10 conference, which boasted football heavyweights like the University of Southern California and its 11 national championships. In 2011, the Pac-10 added two schools to become the Pac-12. Following the 2012 season, four Pac-12 schools finished ranked in the top 25.

Stanford did not lower its standards. Stanford did not seek out easier competition. They didn't even change their uniforms or their mascot! Instead, Stanford made the most important move that any struggling organization can make. They changed their leadership.

In December, 2006, Stanford hired Jim Harbaugh, head coach at the University of San Diego, to lead their football future. A former quarterback in the National Football League, Harbaugh played for 14 years and carried a reputation as a gutsy winner whose teams fought to the final whistle. Fresh off of delivering two consecutive league titles to the Toreros, Harbaugh immediately set about changing the culture surrounding Stanford's team. He hired different coaches, recruited different players, and established a different level of expectations. His leadership produced some of the most successful seasons in Stanford football history. More importantly, though, Harbaugh left a legacy. Harbaugh has since moved on to coach the National Football League's San Francisco 49ers and led them to the Super Bowl in his second year. In their first year without him, Stanford still won 11 games. Stanford University remains one of the best football teams in the country and is ranked as high as number 4 in some preseason college football standings.

I firmly believe that the distinguishing factor between successful organizations and failing organizations is the quality of the organization's leadership. When you think about it, a case can be made that our nation was built on superior leadership. At our nation's founding the patriots faced off against the most educated, farthest reaching, best resourced empire in the world. We won against impossible odds because of leadership provided by heroes whose names continue to reverberate around the world to this day. Leadership is the difference between good and great. Leadership is the key to maintaining a nation, a state, and a community. Leadership is the key to building an effective system of education.

School board members are often asked why they joined the school board. After all, it is a volunteer position that can be pretty unforgiving. Besides the long hours leading up to an election – hours spent knocking on doors and handing out pamphlets – school board service includes late night meetings, conferences, parent complaints, attendance at multiple district events, and the inevitable target that comes with being an elected official. Many people find it difficult to believe that anyone would willingly sign up for that kind of service. And, the truth is, many school board members have trouble articulating why they did sign up.

School board members will say that they wish to make a difference in the lives of children, to insure a better tomorrow, or to leave a legacy. Some will mention global competitiveness or the need to be responsive to the trends that will shape the future. Others cannot find the words to express their interest, but only know that they felt compelled to join the conversation. In the end, the core of the answer is always about leadership. Worrying about tomorrow, leaving legacies, speaking for those who cannot speak for themselves – these are things that leaders do.

Sadly, most school board agendas fail to reflect the fundamental desire to provide leadership. Instead, meetings are littered with the rubble of management. Management has its place, and there are some tasks that must be done only by the school board. However, when these become the focus of the school board's efforts, the board effectively surrenders its responsibility – the responsibility that it was elected to undertake – to other groups. Nobody says that they joined the school board to approve the check register or to evaluate field trips. But, often, these types of activities dominate school board conversation.

School board members should remind themselves – often – of the reason that they joined the school board. Effective, focused, committed leadership can be the difference between tepid results and terrific outcomes. Nature hates a vacuum. When school board members focus on management, they leave a void that others – politicians, administrators, unions, businesses, private foundations, and the like – are only too happy to fill.

These are not the people who were selected to lead and, when they do, the results can be disastrous. In The Essential Drucker, management expert Peter Drucker warns against the dangers of encouraging those without authority to take responsibility for an area. His point is that responsibility and authority are two sides of the same coin. When we give responsibility to a group, that group necessarily seeks authority in order to exercise its responsibility. Unchecked, the result is a power grab. I believe that this is happening in education today because school board members have not adequately addressed the responsibility that their elected authority implies. The battles between and among powerful interest groups are being fueled by our unwillingness to meet our responsibility squarely. It rests with us to check the power grab before it does irreparable damage.

Chapter 3

Do you have a vision for public education?

"Where there is no vision the people perish."
- Proverbs 29:18

Have you ever tried to navigate a crowded room, weaving through tables, chairs, legs, and belongings, while blind folded? Do you think you could do it? Would you even try? Most volunteers faced with this task react in a predictable manner. First, they are incredulous. You want me to do what? Then, they might take a hesitant step, no more than a shuffle. More often than not that initial hesitant step is in the wrong direction. Some might reach out with their hands. Others make helpless noises. Almost all are sure to get some bumps and bruises along the way. Those who succeed in crossing the room will do so slowly and painfully. Most will never cross the room.

A school district without vision is like a blind folded person trying to cross a crowded room. Most districts will never move from where they are today. They will make helpless noises and look with doubt upon the grueling task that they have inherited. Those that do move may shuffle in the wrong direction, paying attention to irrelevant or unhelpful indicators. If, by chance, a district happens to move in the right direction it will often focus too narrowly, reaching out with its arms to avoid crashing into something. No such district survives without bumps, bruises, and scars.

While almost all school districts claim to have a vision for education – even publishing a few words on their web sites or letterhead - most are doing no more than paying lip service to the importance of a vision for education. Few truly understand what a vision is and just how powerful it can be. Part of the problem is definitional. Most people confuse a vision with a mission, limiting the effectiveness of both of these leadership staples.

Consider a hammer. A hammer can be used to do any number of things. A hammer may be used as a paper weight, as a door stopper, as a weapon, as a channel changer, or as a window breaker. I'm sure you can come up with at least ten more alternative uses for a hammer. All of these are legitimate, if questionable, uses for a hammer. None of these, though, are the reason that a hammer exists.

A hammer was created to do one thing really well. A hammer was created to drive nails into wood. In the long and varied history of man, no invention has ever been able to drive nails into wood better than the hammer. The hammer is uniquely suited to meet that particular need. Driving nails into wood is the hammer's mission. Mission statements are statements of purpose. For school boards, they are expressions in the present

33

tense of why we, as school board members, gather on a regular basis. The mission is informed by our answers to questions one and two. What is the purpose of a school board? Why did you join the school board? Combined, your responses form the basis of a mission statement. To simplify, you might remember to start your mission statement with a clause like, "Our school district exists to…"

While a hammer may exist to drive nails into wood, it dreams of loftier things. Indeed, a hammer imagines the wonder of building a beautiful home. This is the hammer's vision. A vision is a statement that articulates a desired future. You might consider beginning your vision statement with something like, "Our graduates will…"

Good vision statements share several characteristics. First, good vision statements are big. That's not to say that they contain a lot of words. Rather, good vision statements articulate a future that causes those who consider it to stop and think for a moment. In fact, the best vision statements are ones that cause a sharp intake of breath because they are so audacious, so unlikely, that they are almost terrifying for those charged with making them happen. When visions meet this hurdle, we quickly realize that there is no way that we would ever be able to make them happen without help. Just as a hammer will never build a beautiful home without the aid of an architect, a saw, a level, and other tools, a good vision causes us to reach beyond the confines of the school board to embrace citizens, businesses, and other community stakeholders.

Great visions do not need to be filled with a lot of lofty vocabulary. In fact, the best visions are ones that are simple to understand and easy to remember. In their simplicity they communicate clearly where an organization is going, the reason it is going there, and the values that will guide them on their journey. Consider these examples:

- "Produce an affordable automobile." – Henry Ford
- "A computer on every desk in every home running Microsoft software." – Bill Gates

These simple sentences serve as ready guidance and inspiration for any who are a part of these efforts. They are big, bold, and easy to understand.

Don't get me wrong – a vision doesn't have to be a one-liner. The important thing is that the vision be clear enough that anyone who reads it quickly understands the challenges entailed. This is critical because a good vision guides every decision, every conversation, that the school board has. This is perhaps the greatest shortcoming of many school districts' use of the vision statement. The vision statement is treated as a procedural necessity as opposed to the foundational element on which all efforts rest. Effective school districts devote considerable time and effort to developing the ideal vision statement for their particular situations. Every word matters because every word will be used to drive behavior in the future. Those vision

35

statements are then internalized, becoming more than a web site banner. They are memorized by stakeholders at every level of the school district's organization. The mission statement is aligned to the vision. Goals are aligned to the vision. Agendas, curriculum, facilities, and budgets are aligned to the vision.

Vision statements are not static. They necessarily change over time, especially as a community changes and the leadership of the district changes. Every leader must be completely invested in the vision. This means that effective school districts re-visit their vision and the resulting mission and goals on a regular basis to ensure that it is consistent with the community's values and desires.

An important implication of the need for the vision to reflect a community's values and desires is that the community must share in the vision. The community, in fact, must participate in driving that vision. Consider our efforts to walk across the room while blind folded again. This time, though, someone else – someone who is not blind folded – takes us by the hand and leads us across the room. This is a better experience than we had when we tried to do it alone, right? The person with vision is able to guide us so that we avoid most of the major obstacles and, eventually, we reach our destination. However, if we're honest with ourselves, we didn't really trust the process along the way, did we? We were probably a bit hesitant and, at some points, it got really irritating to have somebody pushing and pulling on our arms. How could we be sure they were leading us in the right direction? And, a couple of times, we did bump into a table and the bruises leave a painful reminder of those encounters.

Some school districts do a great job of establishing vision, but do so in a manner that means the school board is the only group who can see. In other words, community stakeholders are informed of the outcome of the conversation instead of being formative in driving the conversation. So, like the experience of being guided across the room, the community is pushed, pulled, cajoled, and otherwise led to the ultimate destination. Sure, some of these school districts are effective. But, it takes a long time for them to make it. Trust is granted only in small slivers and there are certainly bumps and bruises along the way.

Now, imagine that we removed the blind fold and asked both people to walk across the room. How easy would that be? Obstacles avoided. Wasteful movement minimized. Time to achievement reduced. This is what happens when everyone shares the vision. This is what happens when all stakeholders in a community's education system join together to identify exactly what we expect to get out of our efforts to teach our children.

Establishing the vision, then, should be the single most important task that a school board undertakes. Properly viewed, the vision sets the terms for how a school district will gauge its progress and define its success. As a community tool, the vision serves to unify stakeholders in a common walk. As a guide, the vision enables the school district to confidently step in the right direction as it pursues educational excellence.

And, the vision is the exclusive province of the locally elected school board. This means that the power to unite, the power to guide, and the power to evaluate rests with local leadership.

Chapter 4

Does what you measure matter?

"Never mistake activity for achievement."
- John Wooden

Sisyphus is one of the greatest villains of Greek mythology. The founder and king of Corinth, Sisyphus routinely found himself at odds with the gods. Among his many transgressions, Sisyphus ran afoul of Zeus by routinely killing visitors and guests, plotting to murder his brother Salmoneus, revealing the hiding place of one of Zeus' concubines to her father, and trapping the god of death in the underworld. After years of treachery and deceit, Sisyphus was finally condemned to a life of useless effort and frustration. His punishment, rolling a boulder up a hill only to have it slide back down the slope as it neared the top, forms such a compelling image that the word "Sisyphean" has come to mean an endless and unproductive task.

For many school board members, the accountability movement of the last thirty years has amounted to a Sisyphean task. Launched shortly after the 1983 publication of "A Nation at Risk," the accountability concept reached its apex with the 2001 passage of the No Child Left Behind Act. This controversial piece of federal legislation requires, among other things, that standardized tests be used to evaluate the adequacy of education received by all students. If student achievement, as measured by the standardized test, is deemed unsatisfactory, a school may be subject to sanctions up to and including closure or reorganization under a privately owned company.

On the surface, the accountability movement would seem to be a good thing. After all, who doesn't want their schools to be accountable for reaching certain minimal standards? This is, perhaps, why "accountability" remains one of the most enduring buzzwords in education leadership. In actual practice, though, accountability has often meant confusion and complexity. One source of complexity is data overload. School board members are called upon to wade through reams of data, ranging from standardized test scores to drug and alcohol violations, and to translate this data into meaningful conclusions that can be used to formulate sensible policies. Sadly, this effort has become Sisyphean in many respects. A typical school report published by the Texas Education Agency's Academic Excellence Indicator System will include 60 or more distinct metrics across 15 categories of students. The full report can easily provide more than one thousand statistics. Expand this to multiple schools per district and add in meaningful comparison groups and it is easy to understand that many boards find themselves awash in so much data, much of it unconnected and difficult to correlate to actual educational results, that they spend hour upon fruitless hour pushing a paper boulder up a very steep, very long hill. If they are lucky enough to glimpse the summit, the paper slides to the bottom of the hill.

Aware of the challenges awaiting all who dare to wrestle with the mountain of data, school boards resort to formulaic approaches to system appraisal in hopes of making their task more manageable. Who is not familiar with SMART (specific, measurable, attainable, relevant, time-bound) goals? Still, given the relative lack of progress in recent history, one must question whether we are really able to identify and measure those things that really matter.

One school district in Texas provides a perfect example of good intentions gone awry. Eight years ago, this district set out to develop an objective appraisal system for its superintendent. Over the course of several months, and after many animated conversations, the board produced what it thought of as the perfect appraisal instrument. In keeping with the SMART mantra, the instrument had seven very specific goals against which the performance of the superintendent, and by extension the progress of the district, would be measured.

Surprisingly, for the next three years, the school board struggled each time it attempted to assess the superintendent's performance. Despite all of their hard work the appraisal instrument did not allow them to answer the key questions about whether they were getting any closer to realizing their vision. After much agonizing soul searching, the board turned again to the appraisal instrument and identified the problem. While the instrument had only seven items, those seven items were measured against literally hundreds of metrics. Indeed, item number one alone was measured against fifty-seven individual metrics.

The district had identified the boulder, and it was massive.

Even when a district is able to overcome the boulder of big data, it may struggle to craft a consistent strategy from the conclusions. Exhaustive data analysis was not required to understand that Eastside Memorial High School in Austin, TX was not succeeding. The school seemed doomed to failure almost from its beginnings, when it was opened as the Albert Sidney Johnston High School in order to serve the African American and Hispanic students of the Texas capitol. You read that correctly. A school to serve minority students was named for a Confederate general!

Thus began a long and troubling history of well-intentioned but botched efforts to hold school leadership accountable. These efforts included turning Johnston into a magnet school for liberal arts (1987), merging the liberal arts magnet academy with a science academy (2002), closing the school down (2007), re-opening the school with a new name (2008), splitting the student body into two schools housed on the same campus (2009), hiring a charter provider to manage the re-merged school (2011), rescinding the charter provider's contract (2012), and entering a partnership with Johns Hopkins University to provide management training and curriculum (2013). The sheer number of reform efforts at Eastside, each motivated and informed by the accountability movement, suggests the absence of a unifying principal around which to build education strategy.

While Eastside may be an extreme case, many school boards find themselves with some version of this malady. This affliction means that school boards may work for hours and days and months and years attempting to craft an educational strategy only to find that they get no closer to seeing the meaningful improvements that they so ardently desire. Instead of achievement boards are saddled with endless activity. Worse, the board's endless activity is amplified across the entirety of a school system, needlessly harming the very people that the school system is designed to support – the students.

It doesn't have to be this way. In fact, the board is possessed of the one tool that can inspire focus – the vision. Rather than become paralyzed by data, the school board should instead ask whether and how each strand of data supports progress towards the vision. Much of it, to be sure, will be deemed applicable. But this sort of rigorous testing will place the data that is kept into its proper context and provide clues as to how it should be used to develop a productive and sustainable system of performance management. Some of the data, though, will be extraneous. In that case, it can be and should be purged as counter-productive.

While it may be clichéd, in the end, a school board's guiding principal must be whether the data drives decisions that are good for kids. On April 17, 2013, the West Fertilizer Company experienced a fire and explosion that devastated the town of West, Texas. In addition to the loss of lives and homes, the blast destroyed two schools. The school board of West Independent School District faced a number of incredibly difficult and important decisions in the aftermath of the devastation. Among the more controversial of these was the decision the school board made to re-sod the field at the high school football stadium in time for the August start of the high school football season. Re-sodding the field had nothing to do with statistics. The field is unlikely to drive improved standardized test scores in any way. But, the school board recognized that high school football meant normalcy for the students of the district. Their decision will never show up on any accountability matrix, but it was the right one because it kept a single unifying thought – what is right for kids – at the forefront.

The reality is that school board members are busy individuals. We are volunteers and, as such, we are heckled and harried and have numerous and diverse responsibilities outside of the education realm. We simply cannot afford to be distracted by anything that does not advance our core calling to have a vision for kids. For this reason, the vision must be clung to relentlessly and wielded with zeal to eliminate anything that threatens its timely march. In this way, the board may be relieved of at least a portion of its Sisyphean charge.

Chapter 5

Do you demonstrate commitment to education improvement?

"Ten thousand hours is the magic number of greatness."
- Malcolm Gladwell

Writer Malcolm Gladwell has become one of the world's most popular authors by combining an easy style, a penchant for storytelling, and an insatiable curiosity about the junction of psychology and sociology. Among his works are the best sellers Blink, The Tipping Point, and Outliers. Gladwell subtitled Outliers "The Story of Success." In this book, he explores the characteristics common to those whose achievements allow them to rank among the greatest in their fields. By studying rock star CEOs, athletic legends, computer geniuses, and musical prodigies, Gladwell endeavors to provide a road map to success.

Gladwell begins with the premise that phenomenal success is built upon equal parts native genius and hard work. As he moves through the proof of this thesis, though, he quickly begins to gravitate towards a slightly altered view that suggests that hard work, and a healthy measure of good fortune, is the true differentiator. As evidence, he provides examples of geniuses who never parlayed their gifts into much more than average achievement (i.e. – Chris Langan, "the smartest man in America") and portraits of people whose tenacity enabled them to beat the odds and become superstars.

This second group includes some familiar icons, like the Beatles. Gladwell relates that when the Beatles achieved "overnight" fame in 1964 their core (John Lennon and Paul McCartney) had already been together for seven years. Moreover, their talent was honed in the crucible of the gentlemen's clubs of Hamburg, Germany. In these clubs, the house band was routinely called upon to play incredibly long sessions. John Lennon is quoted by Gladwell as saying that it was not unusual for the Beatles to play for eight hours at a stretch and seven days a week during their time in Hamburg. After a bit of research, Gladwell uncovered that, in fact, the Beatles had played live shows an incredible twelve hundred times before they achieved their first taste of stardom in 1964.

Similar examples can be pulled from the worlds of sports and business. Tiger Woods began playing golf on a daily basis at the age of three. Bill Gates spent hours on a computer terminal donated to his school when he was in the seventh grade. In nearly every endeavor, Gladwell found that those who achieve mind numbing success do so after spending hour upon hour in back breaking labor. In fact, Gladwell found so many such examples that he was able to develop a rule of thumb. His rule of thumb is that it takes 10,000 hours of work in a field before anyone can expect to break through to greatness.

Compare that figure to the typical school board member's experience. Assuming a school board member is elected to a four year term and the board meets twice per month, a school board member has only forty-eight opportunities to ply his or her craft. That's forty-eight chances to articulate a vision, establish accountability, interact with stakeholders, develop strategic plans, and monitor tactical implementation. Forty-eight chances to provide the leadership that makes a lasting impression on the lives of our children and of our communities.

Quite frankly, it's not enough.

This fact leads to three common sense conclusions. First, it is absolutely critical that no time is wasted. Sadly, many boards find themselves spending time on things that are, at best, only marginally related to student achievement. Whether by design or by unfortunate accident, time spent on mundane work-a-day items – items that are interesting but not fascinating – diminish the impact that a school board member can have. Put more sharply, spending time on debates about the colors of the district seal or the styling of the high school's mascot are, at best, counterproductive and, at worst, outright thievery. They rob the community of the leadership that a school board is supposed to provide. More often than not, the vacuum is filled by people other than those best endowed to understand the needs and desires of the local community. Thus, we have pundits and politicians taking primacy of place in the discussions about education reform.

Granted, it is difficult, if not impossible, to clear the slate of all of the mundane. There are some items that a school board is legally bound to address and there are others that popular sentiment or tradition may dictate remain within the school board's purview. That being the case, it is critical that the school board consciously decides to devote extra time to insure that it is addressing the core elements that do matter. In other words, the board has a responsibility to make time – in the form of special workshops, longer regular meetings, retreats, or electronic communications – to provide leadership on issues of student achievement. In many ways, the board is called upon to defy the tyranny of the now, which always threatens to overwhelm our limited resources, by relentlessly bringing discussions back to the board's core purposes and the vision that the board has for education.

Even with this effort, it does not take a mathematician to figure out that no individual board member will ever reach 10,000 hours of service. Does this mean that school districts are condemned to mediocrity? Not at all! The school board is not a collection of individuals. When functioning properly, the school board and the district superintendent are a team. That team can, as a unit, reach the 10,000 hour mark. For example, in Texas, seven school board trustees and the superintendent form a "team of 8." Over the course of a typical four year term, this "team of

8" could achieve 10,000 hours of service if each team member spends an average of four to five hours per week in discussion about or study of some aspect of student achievement and education improvement. Yes, four to five hours a week is no small commitment, especially when board members factor in family, work, and other obligations. However, it defies belief that anyone who would volunteer to serve as a steward of our nation's heritage and culture would balk at such a commitment.

The American distance runner Steve Prefontaine had a habit of running as hard as he could every time he laced up his shoes. Whether in practice or in a meet, whether a lowly qualifier or the Olympic championships, Prefontaine never allowed himself to take it easy or suffered others to lead. Prefontaine provided a clue to the mindset that led to this remarkable habit when he said, "To give anything less than your best is to sacrifice the gift." School board members are granted the gift of touching eternity. The work they do today will echo through the generations and pave the way for the continuance of our culture. If they fail to demonstrate true commitment, as evidenced by allotting meaningful time to consideration of critical dimensions of student achievement, that gift will be sacrificed.

Chapter 6

Do you prioritize leadership development?

"Leaders aren't born; they are made."
- Vince Lombardi

As this is written, the games of the XXX Olympiad have again captured the hearts and minds of fans the world over. There are many who will willingly watch anything – even the most obscure of sports – if it is associated with the Olympic Games. Over the years, the Olympics have given us a number of incredible athletes and unforgettable athletic moments. Nearly everyone can picture Usain Bolt, Carl Lewis, Michael Johnson, and Marion Jones streaking ahead of the field. Who has forgotten Michael Phelps destroying records and Picabo Street flying fearlessly down the side of a mountain? Many of us get chills when thinking about the Dream Team, draped in flags, re-claiming the gold medal in basketball. Those same chills are present when the anonymous cross-country skier gives everything to represent his country, his sport, and himself – irrespective of the race outcome.

One of the most thrilling Olympic achievements, involving one of the most famous athletes in the world, could not have happened without the help of an Olympian who is largely anonymous. In the 2008 Beijing Games, Michael Phelps won an unprecedented eight swimming gold medals. Without a doubt, his accomplishment is one of the most amazing individual athletic achievements in recorded history. Many people forget, though, that three of those eight wins were anything but individual achievements. They were, in fact, team events in which Phelps needed help from three other swimmers. One of those events almost cost Phelps his immortality.

In the 4x100 meter freestyle relay, the United States - despite the presence of Phelps as the first leg - was not the favorite. Instead, France, anchored by former world record holder Alain Bernard, was expected to win. Phelps began the race well but the Americans soon fell behind the French. By the time Bernard dived into the pool, the French had a half body length lead over the Americans. At the turn, this lead became a full body length.

Watching the video of this race still produces gut wrenching moments. It is interesting to hear the remarks of the race commentators. They say things like "the race is over" and "they're not gonna catch him" and "the race is for silver." And, to be honest, everyone watching thought the same thing. Then, with fifty-meters remaining, something incredible happened. The U. S. swimmer began to gain on Bernard. By thirty meters he had closed to a half body length. At ten meters he had pulled even. At the wall, he edged out the French favorite, securing a 0.08 second win and enabling Phelps to continue his quest for record breaking gold.

The anonymous Olympian who produced this memorable moment was the United States' anchor, Jason Lezak. Beyond hardcore swimming fans and Olympics junkies, he is relatively nameless and faceless. But, in that race...in those few seconds...at that particular moment...Jason Lezak found something. He found greatness. He found the greatness that was inside of him.

Lezak's moment of greatness lasted less than fifty-seconds and came at a most unexpected time. Lezak certainly could not have predicted that this would be the moment that he would be called upon to do something transcendent. Indeed, it would have been easy to assume that Phelps would carry the day and that Lezak would only need to be along for the ride.

The most interesting thing about Lezak's performance, then, is that he was prepared to have that type of performance in the first place. His finish speaks to the hundreds of hours and thousands of meters and countless early mornings that he spent in preparing. He prepared exhaustively for one moment – a moment that he could not predict; a moment that he could not guarantee; a moment that was more hope than promise.

This is the way greatness happens. It happens at unexpected times and in unexpected ways. Greatness is not scripted. Those who would achieve greatness must be prepared for the moment when it is possible. Those who are unprepared will miss their window.

Stop and think about that statement for a second. Everyone has a window for greatness. For some, the window is wide and open often. For others, the window is small and open only for a few moments. But, there is a window for everyone. And to take advantage of that window requires that we prepare ourselves for it – to recognize it and then to go through it.

Those engaged in the public education enterprise are assured of opportunities for greatness. Taking advantage of those opportunities requires preparation. Most of those opportunities will demand leadership. And yet, one of the most persistent myths in our society is that leadership is a trait with which we are born. This thinking would suggest that there is no need – indeed, that there is no point to – preparing for leadership. One either has the ability or does not.

This line of thinking is disturbing, at best, and disastrous, at worst. The fact is that the success of any enterprise – a sport, a business, a nation – is dependent on the quality of its leadership. To suggest that leaders are born is to suggest that whether our endeavors succeed or not is simply a matter of luck. Who among us is willing to leave the education of our children to luck?

Happily, we don't have to leave success to chance because leadership can be – must be – taught. In fact, leadership is a skill that is developed through practice and focused discipline. Like other skills, there may be some who are born with traits that make that skill easier to master. But, possession of those traits does not guarantee mastery any more than the lack of those traits condemns one to failure.

Consider those who play the sport of basketball. Without question, those who are born with a genetic predisposition to great height are possessed of a trait that can help one to succeed in basketball. But, being born with the genetic predisposition to grow to seven-feet tall does not guarantee basketball success. Without training and practice in the several skills basketball requires – dribbling, passing, shooting, footwork – a seven-footer is likely to be a mediocre or worse basketball player. Similarly, a five-foot four inch player, properly taught and with sufficient discipline, can become a fantastic basketball player.

Leadership is similar to basketball in this way. Yes, some are born with gregarious personalities or fearless oratory. But, they may not become leaders unless they are taught how to use these traits effectively. And, many of us learn through countless management seminars that even the least gifted can lead given the right circumstance.

This realization suggests that the successful school district is one that invests in developing leadership. Further, leadership development should be prioritized at every level of the organization. Every aid, every teacher, every campus administrator, every central office executive, and every school board member should be steeped in concepts like vision, mission, advocacy, conflict resolution, motivation, and communication. The best school districts insure that this training is emphasized as much as the latest in pedagogical theory and technology implementation. After all, leadership is the ability to articulate a vision and then help others to realize that vision. Isn't this the foundation of education? Aren't we articulating a vision – a vision of what students can and should be as productive members of our society – and then helping them to achieve it?

A few years ago, the Boston Athletic Association gave every finisher of the Boston Marathon a poster. The poster is a panorama of the finish line that shows hundreds of runners exultant after their achievement. Imprinted above this scene is a simple but powerful statement:

"Greatness goes by many, many names."

Greatness sits in our classrooms right now. It goes by names like Johnny and Susie and Juan and Minh. It waits for us to provide a foundation of tradition and a base of preparation. It strives to conform to the standard that was set by those who first settled this land and then made it the envy of the world. Our Lezak moment may happen at any time. That moment will require leadership.

Chapter 7

Is your board united?

"Whatever comes out of these gates, we've got a better chance of survival if we work together. Do you understand? If we stay together we survive."

- Russell Crowe, as Maximus in "Gladiator"

In the 2000 movie "Gladiator," Russell Crowe plays the Roman general Maximus. After a long and distinguished career as a soldier, Maximus wants nothing more than to return to his home in Spain. The emperor, Marcus Aurelius, has other plans. The aged leader is concerned about the succession and has determined that his son, Commodus, is unfit to rule. Aurelius asks Maximus to return to Rome in order to spearhead a dramatic political shift from empire to republic.

Unfortunately, Commodus learns of Aurelius' plans and acts to thwart them. He kills his father and then sets his guard on Maximus. Forced to fight for his life and then to flee, the fugitive Maximus eventually falls into the hands of slave traders who turn him into a gladiator. Now compelled to fight for the entertainment of Roman subjects, Maximus the slave becomes an unlikely inspiration for a deeply troubled nation.

In one of Maximus' first battles as a gladiator, he is chained to other gladiators and released into the middle of an empty arena. The game master seeks to re-enact the Roman victory over the Carthaginian army led by Hannibal. Not willing to leave the outcome to chance, the gladiators are chained so as to make them easy targets for the Roman charioteers. As the warriors fan out in an effort to assess their surroundings, Maximus focuses on a pair of large gates at the opposite end of the stadium. As the gates begin to rise, Maximus addresses his fellow gladiators. He tells them, "Whatever comes out of these gates, we've got a better chance of survival if we work together. Do you understand? If we stay together we survive."

The gladiators' foes pour into the arena. Predictably, a few of the gladiators ignore Maximus' advice, breaking from the ranks, and are quickly dispatched. The majority, though, fall in behind Maximus. Working together, the gladiators win an unlikely victory, the first of many for the hero Maximus.

This powerful lesson has compelling application for school boards on a number of levels. We must realize that a school board is, like those gladiators who joined Maximus in the ring, chained together. No one of us can make a move without the others. We may tug at our chains and attempt to move in a different direction, but in the end we are bound by our ability to coexist with those who serve with us. Our successes can only be realized as a unit. Like the gladiators, those of us who attempt to work independently of the others will either doom the larger group to failure or destroy themselves.

Further, the survival of our school district, of the educational enterprise, and of our society and culture depends upon our ability to work together. Quite simply, we stand a better chance of forming and achieving a vision if each one of us fully participates in a broader unity. Just as Maximus could not have hoped to succeed in this first battle – a battle that was designed to be a bloodbath – without the concerted support of his fellow slaves, a school board member, in isolation, cannot realize true advances in educational achievement.

Indeed, true success results not only from the efforts of the board but also from the efforts of all who are connected to education – administrators, parents, teachers, and community stakeholders. When the board functions as a unit, it is easier to rally these stakeholders to support of a common cause. When the gladiators stood together, the crowd – sensing Maximus' intent – voiced their approval and support for the effort. This same support is required to achieve education excellence.

This is not to suggest that school boards cannot or should not ever disagree. Constructive debate is a necessity if we are to realize breakthroughs that are informed by impassioned and knowledgeable leadership. However, there is a difference between constructive debate and divisive rancor. Too often, boards are torn apart by disagreements that are personal or political in nature. Setting aside these obvious sources of unproductive discord, there are still bitter disputes about issues that are only on the surface, at best, related to the cause of advancing education achievement.

My own school board has been threatened by these sorts of issues. Not long ago we had a very honest discussion about the role of school board members in directing the daily activities of certain members of administration. During that discussion, we reminded each other that the act of joining the school board meant that we had each consciously decided to sacrifice a portion of our ability to act as individuals. In other words, in exchange for our access and unique voice, we had agreed to subsume our personal interests in favor of the interests of the whole.

A board that can and does ensure that debate is concentrated on elements that truly add value to the educational endeavor must then back this focus with a concerted display of unity. Once a decision is reached, through compromise and consensus, it is critical that the board speak with one voice. There is no place for personal agendas in this most critical of leadership tasks. Stakeholders will not rally behind a divided board. And the board needs stakeholders to help execute its vision.

When the representatives of the thirteen American colonies met in Philadelphia in 1776, they brought with them an assortment of needs and desires reflective of their respective communities' values. Some favored negotiation and settlement with the British while others sought full independence. Some emphasized a loose confederation of member states while others wished to function as a unit. As they labored throughout the summer, they engaged in many healthy and passionate debates on issues large and small. None abandoned his principles. But, each knew that the gravity of the colonial cause was such that the world must see that they were each completely committed to the outcome. There would be no room for equivocation. Once consensus was reached, the group had to speak with one voice. Only then would their fellow countrymen and the citizens of the world take seriously the fledgling nation. Benjamin Franklin famously summarized the colonial leaders' feelings when he opined that, ""We must all hang together, or assuredly we shall all hang separately."

Those who would lead education in the 21st century would do well to apply Franklin's admonition to today's efforts. The success or failure of our efforts to improve education hinges on our abilities to break through partisan division and to remain focused on a compelling vision for the future or our society. If we get this right, we ensure that our descendants are equipped to carry a legacy into the next generation. If we fail, through misguided and misplaced disunion, we doom the future to unrealized potential.

Chapter 8

Do you take advantage of your resources?

"A bad workman will never find a good tool."
- 13th century French proverb

Many new school board members, eager to begin making a difference in the lives of the children of their community, experience a stunning disappointment upon claiming their seat on the board. Beginning with their first orientation session, and reinforced by much of the subsequent training offered, board members are told things that they should not do. Board members are admonished to avoid getting involved in day to day management, told to silence their singular voices in favor of group consensus, advised that they do not actually control curriculum, testing, textbooks, teacher selection and retention, or any of a number of other items that they thought they might be able to influence. It can be a disheartening experience and, in many cases, leads directly to the retreat to safety that is characteristic of school board stereotypes and lamented in this book. Buffeted by the blows of naysayers, board members may be excused for clinging to the few areas that seem safely within their spheres of influence.

There are, of course, good reasons for this guidance. The death knell for many school districts is micromanagement by the school board. The superintendent is hired to execute the vision of the school board. He or she must be free to make day to day decisions in support of that vision without fear of being second guessed. The proper role for the school board is to provide oversight to the superintendent. That cannot be done properly in an environment marked by fear and mistrust.

This does not mean, however, that the school board is powerless. In fact, in carrying out its oversight functions, the school board is armed with an impressive assortment of tools. These tools, when used in support of a compelling vision within a leadership framework, are truly transformative. Indeed, they are among the most powerful tools that any local leader could hope to wield.

As we have discussed, the school board is responsible for establishing the vision for the district. It is almost impossible to overstate the power of this tool. An effective vision serves to guide, illuminate, and motivate all who are engaged in education. The vision provides the superintendent with a definitive destination and represents a rallying point for teachers, administrators, parents, and other stakeholders. We forget about the power of vision because it is so often neglected. Few boards re-visit their vision on a regular basis or call upon it to measure the effectiveness of their conversation. Simply addressing this neglect could mean the difference between a district that stagnates and a district that soars.

Beyond this, the district hires and fires the person responsible for delivering the vision – the superintendent. In his seminal work Good to Great management guru Jim Collins argues that the best organizations identify "first who, then what." That is, successful organizations focus on getting the right people in place and then determine what those people need to do. The superintendent's challenge is significant. He or she must translate the board's vision into a set of deliverables that can be acted upon by the myriad of people – teachers, aides, administrators, janitors, cafeteria staff – that make a school district run. It might be argued, then, that the superintendent is the most important single person in the school district. Getting this "who" right sets the tone for all other activities. The board exercises sole responsibility for ensuring that it identifies the characteristics that will enable this person to be a success, determines who among a slate of candidates displays these characteristics, secures the services of the appropriate candidate, and sets the environmental conditions that enable that person to succeed.

The board's work has only just begun when it has hired a superintendent. The board must then monitor whether the superintendent is executing as expected. The tool for this effort is the superintendent's appraisal instrument. This document represents a living embodiment of the school board's expectations. It provides an objective means for the school board to assess whether the school district is making progress towards realizing its vision. It is critical that this is not a stale document. As the district evolves, the steps it needs to take to achieve the vision will necessarily change. This means that the superintendent's appraisal instrument should be reviewed at least as often as the district's vision. In the end, the appraisal is a powerful tool as it allows the board the means to prioritize objectives and to deliver positive feedback about the district's direction. No other patron of the school district enjoys this type of power.

A fourth source of school board power is the allocation of resources via the adoption of a budget. The manner in which resources are allocated provides a key by which to interpret the school board's priorities and sets the terms under which education will occur. It is no wonder that the budget is the tool that has been most consistently under attack by those who would reduce the school board's influence. It is a most visible display of the power that the school board can wield. The school board must be aware of the messages that a budget sends about how seriously it takes its vision.

Most importantly, the school board is the only group among those that would claim to lead education that has direct access to the community. Indeed, school board members are, first and foremost, community members. And, at the end of the day, education belongs to the community. It is for the community – the future that we hope that community enjoys – that we provide a public education. Those who can leverage the community in their decision making and can speak directly to the community about the shape of public education tap directly into the ultimate source of power. Only the school board can claim this access.

In the Disney cartoon *A Bug's Life*, a colony of ants paid yearly tribute to a group of grasshoppers. The grasshoppers realized that the key to controlling the ants was maintaining the illusion that the ants were powerless. If the ants ever realized that they enjoyed superior numbers and powerful tools of resistance, the grasshoppers would lose their advantages. School boards have been convinced, both by the well-meaning but misled and by the more nefarious, that they are powerless. If – when – school boards realize their power – power that is embedded in establishing a vision, hiring and appraising a superintendent, setting the budget, and interacting with the community – there will be no stopping the advances of American education.

Chapter 9

Do you share your vision for education with the community?

"Our lives begin to end the day we become silent about things that matter."

- Martin Luther King, Jr.

Have you discovered the education miracle that is iTunesU? With minimal effort, and in the comfort of your car or during your daily exercise routine, you can access literally hundreds of the best universities in the nation. This ingenious service allows you to study political science at Yale, energy at the University of Houston, and business at Harvard. Or, if you are like me, you might choose to study education at Stanford University.

Stanford University's Graduate School of Education, a leader in education research, has posted a series of guest lectures that focus on the future of our education system. One of those lectures was delivered by Christopher Edley in March, 2007. Mr. Edley served as the dean of the University of California's law school and has enjoyed a long and varied career - in public service, in education, and in private life - as a civil rights activist.

67

His treatise in this particular lecture was, essentially, that education represents one of the remaining frontiers of the civil rights movement.

While the nuances of classism and equal access to quality education are fascinating topics deserving of their own treatment, it was Edley's attempts to draw parallels between the civil rights movement of the 1960s and the education reform movement of the early 21st century that I found more striking. One of Mr. Edley's statements, in particular, sent me scurrying for the history books. Mr. Edley suggests that, during the heyday of the American civil rights movement, the greatest civil rights gains were made when preachers were the leaders of the movement. Further, he argues that civil rights have suffered some of its greatest setbacks when technocrats and policy wonks have assumed primacy in the movement. This, Edley says, is because of the language that the two groups use to talk about civil rights. Preachers talk about values; technocrats talk about policy. While sound policy must underpin whatever changes we hope to drive, policy that is not driven by a vision based in values fails to inspire action.

From this launching point, we might rightly ask a basic question. Who are the "preachers" for education? Who is laying out the set of values that drive educational improvement efforts? If we are honest with ourselves, we can see that this is an extremely difficult question to answer today. Indeed, it seems much easier to identify the "talking heads" who are establishing policy than it is to articulate any unifying vision. In fact, almost all of the conversation that we come across is dominated by policy makers and data analysts. One must look long and hard to find a compelling voice articulating a unifying set of values that advance the education conversation.

If we accept Edley's premise, and on the surface it appears to be at least directionally correct, then answering this question is of critical importance. Unless we can establish the group of "preachers" who can associate improvement efforts with a set of values, we may be doomed to a series of right-hearted efforts that fail because they appeal more to the head than to the heart. Recent experience seems to support this conclusion. Efforts like No Child Left Behind and Common Core sound right. Logically, they might even make sense. But, these efforts and others like them continually fail, in part, because they do not inspire. While their intentions are noble, their incarnations lack heart that resonates with our communities.

Do we, then, have a set of people who are poised to take on the "preacher" role?

To answer this question, we should first take stock of the requirements to hold such a position. In considering these qualifications, we will use Martin Luther King, Jr., the pre-eminent preacher associated with the zenith of the civil rights movement - as a model. The first prerequisite is an overarching understanding of the key issues facing education. This understanding need not be translated as expertise. Indeed, a

69

close study of Martin Luther King, Jr.'s life reveals that he leaned heavily, and quite effectively, on a supporting cast of experts who had spent, cumulatively, lifetimes developing specialties in the field of civil rights. These were lawyers and organizers, teachers and political operatives. Each one of them, in their own way, was much more qualified to claim the title of civil rights expert than was Martin Luther King, Jr. However, Mr. King had the ability to access this expertise and to synthesize it into an umbrella vision that could be used to unite the disparate groups who strived for the same general goals. In the same way, education "preachers" must know how to, and have the intellectual wherewithal to, tap into experts - like career educators, policy wonks, financial wizards, and political hacks - such that they can knit the whole into a unified message.

A message is only as good as its vehicle. A "preacher" must be able to connect to the masses, meeting people in their own environments and using language that puts them at their ease. There can be no doubt that Martin Luther King, Jr. had this in spades. Substantial portions of the black community were built around the church, a forum in which King was imminently comfortable having been raised in that environment and having chosen it as his livelihood. King, then, was able to position himself as "one of the people," a position that made him trustworthy within his target audience. Beyond this, though, King had a knack for expressing himself in ways that spoke to multiple groups on many different levels - emotionally, spiritually, and intellectually. Having advanced both in the church and the academic communities, King was able to marshal language that played equally in whatever surrounding was required. More importantly, King was accepted as a messenger in multiple domains, having developed credibility both in the black and white worlds. Our education "preachers," then, should enjoy credibility with their target audiences, preferably earned by virtue both of achievement and of origin.

A third requirement is a vested interest in the topic. Such an interest incites passion and a commitment to withstand many of the barbs that a long and protracted struggle is bound to prompt. King was arrested, stabbed, sued, and generally vilified at many junctures of his all too short career. Still, in part because of the vested interest that he had in the civil rights movement both as a black man and as the shepherd of a long-suffering flock, King persevered. In our case, only someone who is completely bought in to the notion of education improvement will have the patience required to sustain the fits and starts attendant with this enterprise.

Of all of the groups who claim an interest in education and education improvement, only one would seem to unite all three of these prerequisites - members of local school boards. By virtue of their positions in the education establishment, they have access to any and all experts - professional educators, elected officials, and scholarly research. Because they are generally uncompensated lay people - elected volunteers - they enjoy an affinity with the community and are able to beat back accusations of elitism and narrow thinking. As parents and as citizens of their local communities, they have a vested interest in the outcomes of their efforts. It should be noted that Mr. Edley might disagree with this assessment, having argued that one of the barriers to education improvement is local control. But we might conclude that this is because he has not carried his own analogy far enough.

In the end, Martin Luther King, Jr. was not a member of the cloistered elite - he was a lay and somewhat reluctant recruit to the cause of civil rights. In a word, he was an amateur in the field of civil rights, having been trained in systemic theology. Likewise, local board members are amateurs who are possessed of a unique set of attributes that make them obvious candidates to "preach" the values that should drive education improvements.

Chapter 10

What can you do now?

"The future depends on what you do today."
- Mahatma Gandhi

Public education as we know it in the United States has a history that spans only one-hundred sixty years. In this relatively short span of time, we have built an infrastructure that provides many of the social underpinnings for hundreds of thousands of families each year. We start and end our days by its bells; we mark our seasons by its calendar; we cheer its teams; we celebrate its achievements. In short, the American education system has become embedded as a part of the fabric of our social lives. This is one of its enduring strengths.

This is also one of its greatest weaknesses. We have institutionalized education. We have become beholden to its traditions and wedded to its structure in such a way that evolution has slowed and, in some cases, stopped entirely. Such a cycle is common in the business world, where new ideas are germinated, grown, plateau, and decline. However, in the business world, we allow for the cycle to follow its normal course. Eventually, old models are discarded in favor or newer ones. We move from industry to service to information. Thus, the economy is constantly reinvented and continuously made relevant to the particular needs of society at a particular time.

Education has not been, and could not be, allowed to follow this cycle to its conclusion. Instead, we have created a Frankenstein apparatus that is a blend of older modalities and newer thinking. In some cases, this works. In many others, though, we are left with an unsatisfying experience that is almost universally disliked. To the extent that evolution continues, it happens on the fringes of education - in the charter schools and magnet operations that can never and will never provide for the masses. What was once revolutionary – a free and publicly available education - has become stale and has ceded the role of innovator to others.

Given our tradition bound system, it is easy to wonder whether a person, or a group of motivated people, can really make a difference. Can anyone really change education? Or, do we tilt at windmills when we entertain such a notion?

I believe that people can make a difference. This belief is not rooted in self-delusion or mythology. Instead, it is rooted in one fact that separates the American education system from that which exists almost anywhere else in the world. In the United States, education is governed locally. This means that in every locale a group of motivated, concerned, outspoken citizens controls the means to lead education's renaissance. The local school board is the body that has been designated, by the community, to provide the voice of this group.

Unfortunately, many school boards have lost sight of their capacity to and of their duty to lead the educational endeavor. They may lead in many things that touch education - approving the budget, setting the tax rate, granting easements, building facilities, hiring and firing staff. But, this is not leading education. Instead, this is leading administration.

In this book, I have attempted to define what it means to lead education. Education is the manner in which we pass along our society's values to future generations. To lead education means to define what those values are, to determine the best ways to pass them on, and to delineate how we will know if they have been passed along successfully. To lead education is to know what a graduate should look like and to work to ensure that all participants in public education have a real opportunity to realize that vision. To lead education is to go beyond the exigencies of today and to plan for the future - a future that extends beyond the next election cycle.

Professional football great Peyton Manning once noted that there are two types of people in the world: people who make things happen and people who wonder what just happened. Too many school boards are wondering what happened - to local control, to the education agenda, to the future direction of our nation's youth. It does not have to be this way. It should not be this way. At the conclusion of this volume you will find a simple assessment tool that can be used to begin self-evaluation and board evaluation. Additionally, I have included my contact information. If you need help in starting to determine if your district shares the activities of high performing districts, I invite you to reach out to me. I know many fantastic advocates who would enjoy helping you to enhance your efforts.

The most important point that I hope you take from this work is that you should always ask questions about education. What are we teaching and why are we teaching it? How can we ensure that our students learn what they need in order to meet the myriad purposes of education? Why do you dedicate your time to this effort? Are you getting the results that you expect from your efforts?

Let this be a call to arms. If we are to truly lead education, we must invest in understanding it. We must study its history and its related subjects. We must be willing to challenge ideas and to create a few of our own. We must not be afraid to enter into discourse, to be proven wrong. We must embrace the conversation and understand that our reward is the journey that this exploration starts.

My challenge to board members, my challenge to anyone interested in improving public education, is to start talking. If you are in a board meeting, make sure that you dedicate time both to the administrative and to the educative. If you are not in a board meeting, ask your board members to discuss the topics that will advance an improvement agenda. If you don't know how to do that - if you don't know what questions to ask – ask for help. Perhaps this humble volume can spark an idea. If so, please share it. I would love to enter the conversation with you.

School Board Self-Assessment

This assessment is designed to help you begin the process of understanding whether and how your school board impacts student achievement. The assessment evaluates the board on ten specific behaviors in which highly effective boards regularly engage. You may find it useful to use this assessment as a part of your school board's regular self-evaluation.

	ALWAYS	SOMETIMES	RARELY	NEVER
What is the purpose of a school board? Do you...				
Understand the traditions and culture that define your community?	4	3	2	1
Value policy-making as a means of enhancing teaching and learning?	4	3	2	1
Assist in setting the strategic direction of the district focused on student learning?	4	3	2	1
Insist on open and honest operations characterized by transparency?	4	3	2	1
Focus board initiatives on student learning?	4	3	2	1
Why did you join the school board? Do you...				

Advocate for children?	4	3	2	1
Demonstrate stewardship and trusteeship?	4	3	2	1
Represent the school with unquestioned integrity?	4	3	2	1
Take pleasure in your work and maintain pride for your contribution?	4	3	2	1
Look forward to solving problems and celebrating successes?	4	3	2	1
Are you creating awareness of the need to improve education? Do you...				
Think patrons view you as visionary?	4	3	2	1
Help build partnerships with community, businesses, and government leaders to influence and expand educational opportunities?	4	3	2	1
Cultivate a sense of urgency about the need to drive educational improvement?	4	3	2	1
Encourage all stakeholders to know and focus on the district mission?	4	3	2	1
Celebrate student learning success in tangible ways?	4	3	2	1
Do you apply pressure for accountability? Do you...				
Expect the school's vision, mission, and goals to address directly student achievement?	4	3	2	1
Focus administrative appraisal on student achievement?	4	3	2	1

Align the board operating procedures with student achievement?	4	3	2	1
Measure school and administrative success by student achievement?	4	3	2	1
Do you demonstrate commitment to education improvement? Do you...				
Show resilience in the face of setbacks and down times?	4	3	2	1
Foster innovation?	4	3	2	1
Expect the highest performance from yourself and others?	4	3	2	1
Equitably allocate available resources to support the school's vision and fiscal health?	4	3	2	1
Focus and appropriate portion of board meetings on student learning?	4	3	2	1
Do you provide support for professional development? Do you...				
Strive to enhance your skills through experience, learning, and training?	4	3	2	1
Design board professional development activities from an annual needs assessment?	4	3	2	1
Actively support leadership development at every level of the educational community?	4	3	2	1
Expect professional growth activities to focus on student	4	3	2	1

learning?				
Communicate high expectations?	4	3	2	1
Do you lead from the front? Do you…				
Know your strengths and talents and lead from them?	4	3	2	1
Take personal responsibility for your actions?	4	3	2	1
Encourage calculated risk taking, accepting occasional mistakes?	4	3	2	1
Insist on research and hard data to identify priorities?	4	3	2	1
Support corrective actions when needed?	4	3	2	1
How deliberative is your policy development? Do you…				
Create policies to enhance student learning?	4	3	2	1
Adopt and evaluate policies consistent with the school's vision?	4	3	2	1
Focus your actions on policy making, planning, and evaluation?	4	3	2	1
Recognize the respective roles of the legislature, state board of education, and your board in governance?	4	3	2	1
Does the community share your desire to improve? Do you…				
Encourage systems for seeking input?	4	3	2	1
Have an effective and legal two-way communication system among the board, administration, students, employees, and	4	3	2	1

community?				
Demonstrate a commitment to shared vision, mission, and goals?	4	3	2	1
Communicate the case for change to improve student achievement?	4	3	2	1
Seek community support for innovative student achievement initiatives?	4	3	2	1
What can I do now? Do you...				
Insist on an annual personal and board self-evaluation?	4	3	2	1
Identify promising practices among peers as models for student improvement?	4	3	2	1
Monitor the professional development system for emphasis on student achievement?	4	3	2	1
Facilitate honesty and fair dealing as hallmarks of every board member and employee?	4	3	2	1
Find meaning and satisfaction in your work on the board?	4	3	2	1

Scores:

Total your score for each section and for the assessment as a whole below.

Purpose: _____
(18-20, excellent; 14-17, average; below 14, needs improvement)

Personal decision: _____
(18-20, excellent; 14-17, average; below 14, needs improvement)

Awareness: _____
(18-20, excellent; 14-17, average; below 14, needs improvement)

Accountability: _____
(14-16, excellent; 11-13, average; below 11, needs improvement)

Commitment: _____
(18-20, excellent; 14-17, average; below 14, needs improvement)

Professional development: _____
(18-20, excellent; 14-17, average; below 14, needs improvement)

Leadership: _____
(18-20, excellent; 14-17, average; below 14, needs improvement)

Policy: _____
(14-16, excellent; 11-13, average; below 11, needs improvement)

Community: _____
(18-20, excellent; 14-17, average; below 14, needs improvement)

Readiness: _____
(18-20, excellent; 14-17, average; below 14, needs improvement)

Total: _____
(172-192, excellent; 134-171, average; below 134, needs improvement)

About the Author

Ken Odom is a school board trustee in Tomball, Texas who has a passion for inspiring local school boards to take an active role in defining the education reform agenda. An award winning public speaker, Ken also works to train youth to tap into their leadership abilities. If you'd like to join the conversation, Ken can be reached via various social media outlets.

Twitter: @kodom

e-mail: ken_odom@hotmail.com

Blog: blog.kenodom.com

Made in United States
Troutdale, OR
11/16/2024

24883531R00051